A Poet's Quest for Valid Questions

natashia ~INDY~ easley

Photography by:

Monte Young
thefilthysneakers@gmail.com

natashia ~INDY~ easley
personal archives

Book Cover Design:

Muneer Sudan
masudan12@gmail.com

Publisher

Bonaventure Publishing
yogiecca@yahoo.com

Contact Information:

natashia ~INDY~ easley
ndeasley@gmail.com
205-201-0686

natashia ~Indy~ easley

DEDICATION

I dedicate my first published collection of poetry to my God above. For without His grace, mercy, and love I would not have survived the struggles I write about nor would I have experienced the love that has helped me move forward with this project. It was God who gave me the gift to write and express myself in poetic form and for His gift I am forever and eternally grateful.

I also dedicate this collection of poetry to Real Life Poets, Inc. I thank God for the sight and vision of the people who came before me and saw a need for such a positive and influential organization. Real Life Poets, Inc. has not only helped me grow as a writer but has allowed me to help and inspire others to use writing to confront and move past their own personal struggles. Furthermore, it was John Paul Taylor, founder of Real Life Poets Inc., who encouraged me to start this project.

Lastly, I dedicate this collection to all my like-minded peers who have reawakened the music and art scene in Birmingham, Alabama. It was seeing you all constantly on your grind and making your art visible that inspired me to share my words with the world. To reiterate my appreciation for all the talent my friends on the art scene encase I dedicate a special piece to you all: **"Room full of talent"**

Room full of talent...

standing in a room so full of talent and influence
so full of go-getters and no-quitters
verbal-spitters and word-smithers
i question...
what kind of impact could words from little old me possibly have?
when I've been impacted by some of the very people in this room
when some of the very people in this room help me harness my craft

yet I have more experiences I could share than words I know
to appropriately spit an accurate depiction
to accurately speak of the impact of such an artistic intervention
though it is my intention to dedicate this verbal piece to you
for my appreciation of the impact your art has on me
and influences me to share my words with you

because despite not doing the beats
I appreciate you all taking the time to flow with the words I speak
taking the time to discern what I'm preaching about
allowing me to teach you what the world has taught me
and sharing what the world has taught you
yet you all have taught me so many lessons
to appropriately thank you,
I'd be like the long-winded person no one ever asks to do the blessing
and if you know me,
I'm not into waiting on food

but its only appropriate I give credit
to those who came before us
and made artistic magic a precedent
now the glow of Magic City is omnipresent
and every day the flow of art is present

maintained in the present by Generation Right Now
not Generation Next
because we don't wait our turn
dropping lyrics the mainstream can't discern
but we understand each other
and support each other

promoting each other's dreams
like we sharing dreams

because this scene is a family for us
and I can't spit hard enough
or thank you enough
but after all these lines
I'm sure you get the purpose of this rhyme
so I'll just say again...thank you!

Table of Contents

Foreword

I remember our very first meeting and she walked up and said "Hey, I'm Natashia but they call me Indy and I am a Poet". That day she recited some of her work and I instantly became a fan. I knew I was dealing with something "Special" here. She has been such a blessing to the community by sharing her truths and mentoring with Real Life Poets to be an example for the next generation. She has gracefully taken her life stories and turned them into poetic gifts to stimulate the many senses and that is a skill not easily acquired. And after mentioning several times I knew she needed to let the world read her work. I am proud to see *A Poet's Quest For Valid Questions* come to life, Real Life.

This collection of poems takes you a journey and will have you asking questions of your own life. Who Am I? Who is God? What is Love? Why do I write? What is perception? What really matters? These are all questions that will be explored, analyzed and answered for the reader through Indy's words. She bares her soul and invites the reader to be a fly on the wall in her world. Perfectly placed phrases and descriptions gives you the sense that she took great care and energy in articulating the emotions and message of each poem. One clear message throughout the collection is Hope. The poem *The Role of Hope* speaks directly to my spirit in that I agree we all need it every day of our existence. The lines *" hope is the motivation that keeps us growing/that keeps us wanting to know more/and see more of the view not easily seen/but obtainable when hope accompanies our dreams"* is an example of her always striving, reaching, searching and wanting for more out of this life.

I am honored to see Indy step out on Faith and reap the beautiful harvest of her planting seeds. Indy know that the journey that you have been allowed to take in this life will now benefit and enrich the lives and hearts of the many people that will have the pleasure of reading this amazing collection of poetry. To you my friend I say congratulations on a great first book. I end by saying "Spit Poet!"

John Paul Taylor, Co-founder of Real Life Poets, Inc.

INTRODUCTION

I'm gracious for your interest in my poetic compilation
Now consider your invitation given and accepted
Consider your access granted to my quest
as I seek to remove all that has been previously planted about me.
I am Indy,
Sometimes believed to be the one that deceives you as Tasha
but my birth name is Natashia
yet my mama wanted Nastashia
So thankfully this is not a piece about my name
For this is my introduction
to my personal quest to discern what is a valid question to me.
Beyond just asking a bunch of questions,
to discovering "**Who am I**?" to me
A question I could not answer until
I distinguished "**Who is God**?" to me
Only then could I accept "**What is Love**" to me
And somehow all these questions
were transformed into my pieces of poetry
that I now share with you from me.
Poetry that gives you a look beyond the exterior of my questions
into the interior of "**Why I Write**"
A look beyond what is the exception,
to reflect "**What is perception**?" to me.
All in my quest to answer "**What really matters**?" to me
Me, A 'poet' in my own right,
and this is my introduction to my quest for valid questions.
Though while I was asking all these questions,
I probably should have asked
how do I properly do an introduction?"
But I'm poet and poetry is what I do.
So this piece I dedicate to you
and I hope you enjoy.
Thanks for the support
And for what it's worth,
This poet loves you!

Who loves me? Why me? What is my purpose? Where am I going? Why did that happen? What is love? Is this it? Which direction do I go? Who do I turn to? Does anyone hear me? Does anyone see me? Am I changing? Have I changed? How much have I really grown? Who am I? How important is faith? What really matters? How important is love? Why don't they love me? What is the motive? What is love's purpose? What is a valid question? What is the point of curiosity? What is the purpose of learning? Why do I write? Why did I start writing? Who do I write for? What purpose do I write for? What purpose does my writing serve? What is the lesson? Does age matter? Who is God? What did the experience reveal? Is God real? Can I really be myself? How did society get here? What is perception? What is to become of tomorrow? What does the future hold? Who is going to help the kids? Why do we hate more than we love? What do I want to be? What do I want to accomplish? What will it take to get there? Is the sky my limit? What will I be remembered for? Why do I share my poetry? Who is my inspiration? What is my inspiration? Is it time to let go? How much time do I have left? What do I regret?

What is the meaning of life? What is truth? How do I get to Heaven? Is love ever forever? Am I dreaming? Is this real? What is an illusion? Why am I hurting? Why do I care? Who do I admire? What is a friend? What is the meaning of family? What is fear? Am I afraid or cautious? Why do I pray? Are prayers really heard? Can I love again? How do I forgive? How do I move past the pain? Can I forgive her? Can I forgive him? What is a mother? What is a father? What is success? Where does my peace come from? Why do I smile? Can I trust her? Can I trust him? Why a book?

who am I?

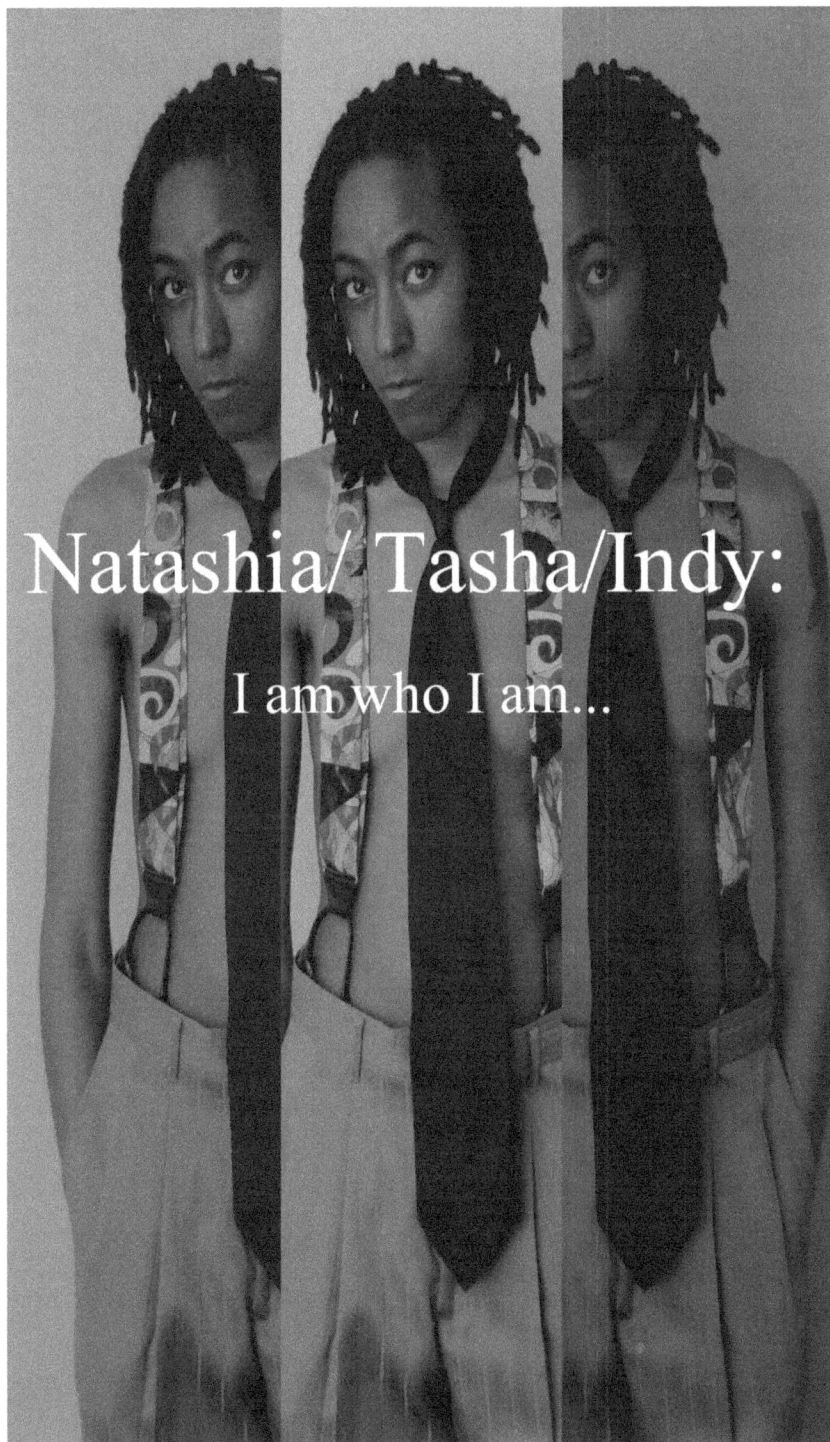

Natashia/ Tasha/Indy:

I am who I am...

Defined...

If I must be defined at this time

or at any time

I ask you to remove any previously held judgments

and make the proper adjustments

so that your mind can be opened

to an original design, which is I

yes I may look quite normal

to the open eyes

but what you don't see

is what is beneath my fleshly disguise

you may see my bruises on the surface

but what you don't see is the roots

what you don't know is my truths

only what you assumed truth to be

only your assumptions make you the ass

and not me

because your story can't define me

despite our said similarities

for I am one of a kind

a rarity in times when

society mocks my originality

labeling me a causality to their traditions

because I petition every rule

I've ever been given

rules that threaten to strip me

of my artistic tools of expression

empty me like the pockets of

those who suffered from the recession

but I can't fit in just one definition
so how can you define me?
when what I am never changes
but who I am never stops changing
keeping me always one step ahead
of your attempts at containment
for if I must be defined at this time
or at any time
allow me to explain me
not a label
allow me to answer your questions
not prewritten statements
found on personality surveys
that supposedly portray an accurate account of me
but if real eyes recognize real lies
how real are you
if you easily believe the gossip
in a world where false rumors
are spread for a profit
and my gayness has been out the closet
yet its still a popular topic
like I'm some fatal toxin
yet I'm not apologizing
nor am I asking for one
I simply ask you stop
your attempts at defining me
for if I must be defined at this time
or at any time
allow me to connect the dots for you

to tell you the difference

between the reals and not so true depictions

allow me to give you

the non-fiction version

the cliff-notes version

if you don't want the long story

because who could be a better

teller of my story than i

for who can define me

if they don't even know why I cry

or the motivation behind

what keeps me trying

for any outside definition of me

is a contradiction to my make up

to what is visible when I'm naked

to when I'm on my knees and

openly confessing

to what is seen when I'm viewed

as my heavenly Father's reflection

to my own held definition

and the only one that should matter

but should can't be could

as long as wannabe prophets

or simply know it alls

contend to know it all

yet my heavenly Father does

still I hold no grudge

for your previously held conclusions

because i too get lost in the

confusion of definitions

but i am no ruse

or figment of your imagination

only the lies you've been told

are imagined

and it's the definitions you hold

that are inaccurate

so if I must be defined at this time

or at any time

allow me to define myself

Don't judge me...

there is only one universal request

I ask of this world

to simply let me be and love a girl if I want to

I ask to not be judged for who I love

to have no grudge held against me

to not smudge me with opinions

or bind me with a petition

to stay within marital traditions

that exclude me

because society labels my love as a condition

a selfish complex I have to be different

because others have changed

and now society is convinced we are all the same

so attempts are made to tame my lifestyle

and chain me to alternative views

certain I can choose what to feel

not understanding how many like me

would rather kill themselves

than face the chilling stares of homophobes

like themselves

but I can't change myself

even if I tried

because I did

as many nights I cried out to God

to take away this burden

yet He spoke to me

and assured me everything I am

is all within my purpose

and that I'm not only beautiful just as I am

but my spirit is gorgeous

and one day all this suffering will be rewarded

and I will be rewarded for simply being me

as I am

so I ask that you not judge me

because I am who God has chosen me to be.

Am I Better?

you ask me if I think I'm better than you

my answer is a simple no

but I know better so I do better

so if in doing better makes me better

then my answer should be yes

but I detest the need to speak

continuously highly of myself

for if I'm left as simply Indy

there is no need to compete with anyone

for I only desire to be better than myself

better than material wealth

better than infinite riches

better than the visible self

better than the best I can be

by simply being I-N-D-Y

I don't have to try to be me

already motivated to be better

by what I see when I view the world

with a desire to conquer

with a hunger to learn

and discern the hidden mysteries

to satisfy my mental curiosities

of what it means to succeed

and really be the best that I can be

driven by what I can't do

by what they say I won't do

or couldn't, or shouldn't do

by what I thought I knew

that I didn't

yet self-improvement only comes when committed

to learning what is better

so I can do better

from the knowledge experience teaches

from the right doing wrong preaches

from the depths of my soul words reach

life teaches me daily

the right and wrong way to be

so by simply opening my eyes

and refusing to accept disguises

I discover in myself

the secret to what makes me better

but not better

it's simply because I know better

that I do better

so if that makes me better

then my answer is a clever yes

Curiosity...

they say curiosity kills the cat but I'm still alive

but if it's a true statement,

I ask that this cat get 9 lives to live.

because where I'm concerned, the only thing a healthy curiosity kills is ignorance.

and since I never been one to hear something and just go with it

I'll take my chances at landing on my feet if I were to fall from the mountain peak I'm climbing up.

and will get up eventually.

because defeat is not an option and road blocks are only temporary obstacles

while questions are more important than the answers I seek

because the search is when seeds are sown in me

and the quest itself is what teaches the lessons that better me

so I can be a better me.

otherwise, what's the point of curiosity?

if not to expand and enhance oneself

I'd simply be overwhelming myself with irrelevance.

without a question, I'd be moving without directions.

without a destination, I'd never get anywhere worthy.

I'd die ignobly.

so I rather know what's worth knowing than knowing everything

because everything is not good to know

and not everything helps me grow

leaving sown seeds to never grow.

so judge me by the questions I ask rather than my answers

because I don't know if I have the right answers

but mostly because the questions themselves answer any questions this world could ask about me

while my curiosity allows me to continue to discover me

as I move forward,

opening new doors

and doing new things

because if curiosity killed the cat,

only self-satisfaction can bring him back alive

back to that 2nd life with a new chance to strive for perfection

or just striving for direction

yet it all starts with a question

because curiosity is the first and simplest emotion we ever evoke

though for the open mind, perennial curiosity lingers on

like freewheeling intelligence that continuously defies excellence

and levels any and all pre-held expectations

In the search for a difference between

relevant and tangential questions

The Overachiever

I'm the overachiever with dreams I can believe in
never believing I had dreams I couldn't succeed in
hesitating only momentarily in the face of fear
I propel myself forwardly with blind ambitions
making the personal decision to fuel my own visions
which is a complete derision away from statistics
that fail in their predictions of me
because I'm simply I-N-D-Y
the one thing I don't have to try in
and no one has to buy in
because I'm a Gemini twin type
but only in hind sight
because stars so bright couldn't shed light
on who I am with the lights on
or off for that matter
because I'm quick to shatter any varieties of me
being nothing short of phenomenal
phenomenal woman I am
just the way I am
without the dresses
and a neck full of necklaces
I'm artistically reckless
even in the way I dress man
but I'm not a man
or a girl playing dress up
or intentionally covering her chest up
breast is just something that never came
but I'm a woman who loves women one in the same
with black skin and white friends
because I don't pretend to fit in racial cliques
that further ignores the very ideals my ancestors died for

despite being the receiver of racism
no different than men's sexism
I live for the promotion of acceptance
believing difference isn't worthy of rejection
so I'm objecting any notion of exclusion
and introducing myself into the discussion
of forward thinking, forward progression
and to reject me is to accept regression
because I've come too far to be silent now
but I have to actually bother now
so I pick up a book to enrich my mental
because knowledge is everything but simple
but free to me, the overachiever
the receiver of a degree
despite the adversity to get it
I ignored the idea I couldn't get it
now I'm back at it..
to be a master of my craft
the poetic professional
giving the world an open confessional
of an overachiever
willing to reach beyond my grasp
beyond my past
beyond the stereotypical tasks
assigned to my gender
I'm a bender of the rules
and not a pretend celebrity
rather I'm Indy every day of the week
and no one has to like how I do me
so if you don't then sue me
to satisfy your monetary greed
that I won't no part of

because I'm not that hard up
rather I do good deeds because it's me
because it's free
and because of the need I see
when I open my heart to more than just me
striving to live my life unselfishly
and gratefully for all that I am
and will be
so I accept control of my destiny
and refuse to settle for anything less than the best of me
so yeah, you can call me an overachiever
yet you don't have to be a believer in me
just trust & believe I will be on the receiving end
of what it means to have dreams you can succeed in.

Gifted...

I was informed around 5 years old that I was gifted

and I didn't really get what was meant at the time

so I smiled and went with it

I heard words like smart and intelligent

excelling and better

but I noticed the sneers and dirty looks more

because my peers didn't seem to agree with the teachers

and it seemed like more work was asked of me from my teachers

so I purposely failed my academic assessment

thinking no test was worth losing friends over

and I could focus on school when I got older

so the gifted program passed me over

not once, but twice

and I was left with less cold shoulders than before

only to learn as I got older

the only one who got passed over was me

and playing dumb didn't get me accepted

and it didn't please my grandma either

so after that first F got me an A+ beating

I started exceeding what was expected of me

to give learning the best of me

and though some of my peers berated me

none of them are here to celebrate success with me

so now I'm finally understanding what it means to be gifted...

but more so what it means to exceed for your own benefit...

yet I still smile and simply go with it...

The rush to grow up...

now that I'm grown I don't have many regrets

because each one taught me one

and I just did and do my best to learn something from it

but I promise I do have this one regret

and it's the rush I was in to grow up

because if I could go back and see the little me

I'd tell the little me to shut up

and take back those foolish statements

because now that I am grown, i regret those statements

statements like...

"I can't wait to be grown"

"I can't wait to leave home and move out on my own"

"I can't wait until I can do what I want to do"

and have no one to answer to

but that was obviously before I really knew what I wanted

because now that I'm grown, its all this responsibility I don't want

now I just want to go back to my younger days

when 1+1 still equaled 2

and x didn't equal a number

or perform some function I still can't remember

back when my first choice of the day was honey nut cheerios or fruit loops

and there was time outs for not telling the truth...

or even back when the hardest question I had to answer was whether my birthday made me a Gemini or a Cancer

and i was too young to even know the correct answer

but back then i thought i knew all the answers

and the last person i was trying to listen to was my parents

especially when they were barking out demands

to do the dishes and clean my room up

or screaming to wake me up for school

or screaming to remind me of some household rule i failed to comply with

which made being a kid something i hated

and i begin counted down the days as early as the fifth grade

because i just knew i was ready to be older than my age

but now that i'm grown, it's my younger days i miss

and i regret my persistence

and know-it-all insistence that i knew it all

i regret my rush to grow up

and all those times i wished those adults would just shut up talking to me

because i thought surely they didn't understand a kid's struggle

surely they didn't understand the troubles a kid faced

but now that i'm grown

i'd just as surely do an about face just to be a kid again

because if i could do it all over again

i promise i wouldn't complain as much as i did

i promise i wouldn't have been rushing the way i did just to grow up

and i'd happily tell the little me to shut up

just to not have these grown people problems just yet

and not have the rush to grow up be the hardest regret i now have to ingest

Explosive emotions...

by the time i entered adulthood, i didn't recognize myself

because the person in the mirror resembled my reflection

but appeared to be more so a deflection of the me i was meant to be

but could never see

because real eyes had failed to realize i had been wearing a disguise all this time

see as time passed on,

i hid even more of myself

until i begin to die inside myself

left with a person i didn't want to know

and didn't know

because my lies by omission had kept the make-up of my inner being a secret

and the deepest of my emotions were hidden even from myself

i had conceded to the notion the real me was too weak to speak my truth

and in retrospect, i was then defeated by the same notion

replacing my reality with imaginary fallacies

in an attempt to shield myself against any further tragedies

and stop the pain before i became a casualty of myself

but before i could return to the ashes of myself

my emotions exploded

and my anger imploded inside of me

and it was anger that became me

and my non-forgiveness that would change me the most

anger from knowing those i loved the most had drained me the most

thus for, the sweet girl was sweet no more

loved no more, felt no more than what she wanted supposedly

when what i really wanted was a father who kept his promises

and didn't make it out to be a bother to keep up with me

what i wanted was a mother who wasn't always beating on me

and speaking down to me

what i wanted was a mother and a father who loved me for me

but i convinced myself wanting was pity seeking

and pity was for somebody else

because i had emptied myself until there was nothing left to feel

no more of myself others could steal from me

like my innocence he stripped from me when he ripped trust from me

when his occasional nightly visits disrupted the child in me

like my ability to forgive she took away from me each time she berated

then loved me in the same day

but it would be what i had to say about it all that saved me from it all

when one day what started as an ink stain set in motion an attempt to explain my pain from its roots

i begin to write to explain my truth

to drain my truth before it drained me

to stain my paper with ink from all the pricks that permanently stained me

i used ink to stain my paper with words to explain a me i didn't know

and hadn't known in a while

hadn't seen since i was a child

and hadn't been around for a while

but i would smile more as words became my addiction

and i learned to separate my truth from my fiction

learned to accept the bruises from my afflictions

and use them to my benefit

my explosive emotions would no longer be my nemesis

but the premises on which i discovered me

and discovered how poetry could further help me explore myself

channel myself

and love myself

without hiding myself

Disadvantage of being me...

i was born with several stereotypical disadvantages

yet i learned early on to use them to my advantage

so even in present day, i refuse to give away the advantage i gain each time i defy normalcy

each time someone attempts to challenge the balance of my being

because i am completely ok with being the minority, even if i have to stand alone

while the majority seems to be completely ok with complacency

but i will never be okay with complacency

because there is so much more i desire to be

because my words without action are a complete disgrace to me

a total waste of me

and the abilities that make me

abilities i have acquired through persevering through countless struggles

and standing firm at the sign of countless troubles

because my troubles never last always

but the lessons learned from my troubles last always

and unfortunately i've learned more from bad days

than i've had good days

sometimes finding it difficult not to stray from my journey

yet i never lost sight of my journey

may have been discouraged by obstacles on my journey

but thus far i've conquered the obstacles of my journey

encouraged to turn my shortcomings into my forthcoming moments

and elevated through an increase in my drive during my toughest
moments

because i've survived the worst of situations

and came out better because of the situations

despite the wavering of my motivation from time to time

i've held on and continued pressing forward each time

so i'll continuously decline any notion i'm at a disadvantage

because tough times haven't defeated me yet

instead tough times have strengthen me

encouraged me

empowered me

to simply be................me.

Stumbling...

confused,

i've been aimlessly wandering,

somewhat stumbling

returning to old lessons already learned

reflecting upon bridges now burned

trying to discern the intentions of lingering shadows...

Sleepless nights...

on those sleepless nights i sometimes wish i could hide from the very sight of myself

ashamed of what i see

but can't see as i allow the darkness to consume me

all alone i cry for me

for the need to sleep deeply

without the fear of creeping

or hearing the screaming again

on those sleepless nights i just want peace

and an end to the nightmares that keep me awake...

Loving myself...

i once forgot how to love myself

and consequently, my real self got lost amongst my shadows

i had never intended to lose myself

only change myself

but when the transition was complete

i no longer recognized the girl i always knew as me

she looked like me

and talked like me

but she wasn't me

i had become this girl everyone else wanted to see

despite how damaging it could be to my soul to hide myself

i discarded my pride and all that was left of me for others

when once i prided myself on my ability to not care about what others think

only to later in life get caught up in what other people think

so i made this change and stepped outside my usual range of comfort

only to find myself suffering from the discomfort i was feeling

from my attempt to be someone my soul wasn't willing to be

because i had stripped myself of more than comfort found in clothes and style

instead, i had ripped from myself the true identity of indy

becoming a nonentity when i agreed to the conformity of details that define my gender

i became a pretender of myself

when i gave up my right to be a defender of myself

when i took away the me that was a reflection of my life itself

instead i reflected what's left when the soul departs the flesh

suggesting i was dead alive

and each night my soul cried out for me

to defy the beliefs of others that attempted to bound me

to a stereotypical representation of who others thought i should be

and i allowed it

allowing their tone to grow louder than my voice

allowing their choices for me to drown out that which was once me

the me i loved

the me God loved as is

yet the real me had been clouded by their religious attempts to imprison me

and condemn me for being me

they questioned the solidity of my faith because of who i laid with

and consequently, it would be their opinions that dictated my fate

when once i had taken a stand against mere opinions

against conditions that threatened my position to be myself

i used to stand by my vision to be me despite common verities of society

yet i too became a follower of austerity

allowing insularity to overcome me

until my mirrors no longer reflected the me i once was

but thank my father above for showing me the path back to His love

for encouraging me to rise above the prophets of false prophets

and shatter all those mirrors that no longer reflected me

and disregard all those opinions that did not project me

and turn a deaf ear and blind eye to gender conformity

because only then could i find my way back to me

a dead alive reflection emerging from the shadows

lost but found again

ending the need to pretend i was someone i could never be

because when i found me

i discovered i could not disregard who i am for others

only then did i fully recover for losing myself

and truly learned how to be faithful by loving myself

Born This Way

Times...

despite how dark my times get, i find it harder to quit

and almost impossible to sit still

while time keeps ticking away

for my struggles have produced plenty of bad times

making me no stranger to difficult times

seemingly always in search of better times

yet i accept it may all be just a product of current times

because time does not wait nor stop for me

nor does time pity the fool who lives with regrets

and continuously second-guessing decisions that past times reflect

because past times are lost times

with no rewind option to redo the bad times

with no reward for holding on to the once good times

making the present time the only relevant time i got

so as i embark on this journey

i am committed to making my present time my best times

instead of time defining me based on past times

for it was time that took away my dark times

and it was my dark times that taught me to appreciate all time

for bad times are an equal teacher to good times

and only with time can i grow into a sound mind

with enough knowledge to navigate the bad times

and appreciate the good times of the current times

for troubles don't last always

but lessons learned from troubles last always

so i accept my good times along with my bad times

and embrace my most difficult times as my maturing time

by sowing better seeds for better times

because time is all i got until the end of time

yet time doesn't wait nor stop for me

so i make the most of the current times

because my present time is the only relevant time i got..

Dear indy...

i want to start off by saying i'm proud of you

if no one is proud of you, be assured i am

because i am those emotions you experience within yourself when troubled times find you

so i know exactly how explosive i can be

i know how many times a week you cry yourself to sleep because of me.

i know how many times you don't eat because of me

but i also know how strong you can be because you always seem to defeat me one way or another

even when my explosive eruptions land you in more trouble than you started with,

time after time you may bend but you haven't broken yet

and lately, you haven't allowed me to erupt as much

while normally, i'd erupt at just the thought of being held in

but you've found a way for us to co-exist as friends rather than frenemies

because i still get my passion filled releases

and you in turn transform them into understandable thesis statements

giving me, your emotions, a platform to be savored

and i in turn wage less wars against you

favoring peace agreements

over lingering misgivings of others

i commend you for learning to adapt

because we can't exist without each other

and truth is, you can't be you, if we don't have each other

so i just wanted to express my gratitude for the transformation your attitude has been through

even if no one else notices,

i know you're not the same young girl with the short fuse temper

or the girl who could hold a grudge through 5 decembers

but you're also no longer the emotionless pretender

nor the emotional avenger

instead, you've managed to find a balance
and though every day it's a challenge
you're better today than you were before
and i do notice
so i encourage you to simply keep your focus
and ignore those who are turning noses up at your change
because your path holds possibilities only you can expand
and i see it firsthand how much you're capable of withstanding
i've seen firsthand how much you're changing for the better
and i know how good me and you can be together
when i'm channeled through your expressions
and my confessions are controlled
behold, you are now a new being with a purpose who is learning how to properly channel her emotions
and know if no one else notices, i do

sincerely,
    your explosive emotions

Who loves me? Why me? What is my purpose? Where am I going? Why did that happen? What is love? Is this it? Which direction do I go? Who do I turn to? Does anyone hear me? Does anyone see me? Am I changing? Have I changed? How much have I really grown? Who am I? How important is faith? What really matters? How important is love? Why don't they love me? What is the motive? What is love's purpose? What is a valid question? What is the point of curiosity? What is the purpose of learning? Why do I write? Why did I start writing? Who do I write for? What purpose do I write for? What purpose does my writing serve? What is the lesson? Does age matter? Who is God? What did the experience reveal? Is God real? Can I really be myself? How did society get here? What is perception? What is to become of tomorrow? What does the future hold? Who is going to help the kids? Why do we hate more than we love? What do I want to be? What do I want to accomplish? What will it take to get there? Is the sky my limit? What will I be remembered for? Why do I share my poetry? Who is my inspiration? What is my inspiration? Is it time to let go? How much time do I have left? What do I regret? What is the meaning of life? What is truth? How do I get to Heaven? Is love ever forever? Am I dreaming? Is this real? What is an illusion? Why am I hurting? Why do I care? Who do I admire? What is a friend? What is the meaning of family? What is fear? Am I afraid or cautious? Why do I pray? Are prayers really heard? Can I love again? How do I forgive? How do I move past the pain? Can I forgive her? Can I forgive him? What is a mother? What is a father? What is success? Where does my peace come from? Why do I smile? Can I trust her? Can I trust him? Why a book?

who is God?

God:

The creator and ruler of the universe and source of all moral authority; the supreme being

Scars...

for she wears scars no one sees
invisible
...to eyes wide closed.
for she is predisposed
to internal bleeding
from all the beatings
that only pure evil
could inflict
like conflict diamonds,
her star shined bright
but never in alignment
when she needed it the most
as most days saw her
struggle for survival
as her troubled soul went unnoticed
because eyes wide closed
was those very eyes
that see not what is not desired to see
when it is much easier
to generalize rather than sensitize
the coldest eyes to her reality
it was then she lost focus
amongst the coldest shoulders
while choking back her frustrations
with every closed mind
that attempted to cage her
when once it all enraged her
and her emotions enslaved her
she hit the bottom
and the reality of her stagnation
saved her

saved by His grace
and the mistaken perception
she lived for expectations
that weren't her own
her praise now goes to Him most high
and Him alone
the only king upon a throne
who can judge her
yet others still judge her
and while she is aware of the whispers
and hears the difference in opinions
when she is the topic of conversation
she waits for no invitation
as she makes the boldest of declarations
that her life is too worth saving
and she can and will be saved
from the harsh realities
she faces daily
all while saving face
yet make no mistake
while her anger once misplaced her
it was God's love
that once again found and saved her
and He forgave her
as she forgave herself
knowing God makes no perfect beings
and there is always new beginnings with Him
she now declares her victory
before each battle
because her triumph is inevitable
even as she bleeds
without the presence of an open wound

and continues to suffer
she is now guided by His light
a blinding sight
that no longer goes unnoticed
she now beats her own drums
toots her own horns
sounds her own alarms
upon her entry
waiting not for an invitation
as she's no longer waiting for approval
spiritually lifted by His removal
of the ability to consider
opinions that never mattered
nor improved her circumstances.
for God is the only giver of her second chances
and His light enhances each scar
for it was when she could
only see flaws and scars
that God called what He saw her beauty marks.

Impact of forgiveness...

inside me is a heart
that has been repeatedly pounded
yet it still manages a beat
even when in close proximity
to what should be sure defeats
my heart just keeps beating
sometimes at the faintest pace
other times the beat is rapid
spiked by memories of moments
i can't seem to forget
and i can't seem to forgive either
instead bitterness stirs up my blood
and keeps me from moving forward
keeps me from obtaining any
sense of order of my emotions
as i'm the only one choking
refusing to fully swallow
previously stripped innocence
by the very ones i thought
could never evoke such rawness
but i thought wrong
or was i wrong to think
love meant you wouldn't hurt me
nor desert me
or touch me inappropriately
now i'm told i'm supposed to forget
so that i can forgive
the misgivings done to me
but when sleep avoids me
and the noise is turned off
i lie still as if in a coffin

often replaying the past
like a broken record
like an unwritten bestseller
i fail to live up to my potential
held back by my own unforgiveness
and stubbornness
but the only one still hurting is me
hurting myself each time
my emotions explode
each time i expose myself
when angry
when pain drains me
and the inflictions leave permanent stains
on my resume
i'm the only one that appears deranged
and unable to contain my own emotions
despite for some events i wish i wasn't chosen
but i was
and i am who i am because i was supposed to go through it all
and i may not know all the reasons
but God explains with seasons
the need for growth and change
so i'm growing from never forgiving
to appreciating the misgivings done to me
for it is what i have been through
that has made me who i am
now proud of the scars
visible and unseen
proud of the screams that wake me up from nightmares that threaten
to consume me
proud of the words that tell of what once threatened to consume me
but failed
because i forgive others just as i forgive myself

i, an imperfect being striving for perfection
i, who lives for love and its connections
with a for better or worse
miss one, next one mentality
i have to be apologetic of myself
if my process is to turn into progress
i can't allow any mistake to remain one
even if i commit the same one multiple times
i have to keep trying, striving, forgiving myself
i have but little choice left
for forgiveness is the engine that drives the beats in my heart
slowed down only by old grudges and inflammatory emotions
that aren't let go of
so i forgive
because my heavenly father forgives me
so i forgive
because the only one it hurts is me
so i forgive
because it is the only way i can honestly declare i live.

Illusions...

i found myself face to face with so many illusions,

i begin to question daily how do i keep from losing it

and from drawing conclusions before the moment itself is experienced

how do i maintain my balance

when everyday poses its own share of challenges?

when every day comes with disappointments and even more broken promises?

how do i cling on to faith on days when my hope is misplaced?

only to search my own face in the mirror for what's real

and not recognize the reflection of what i really feel inside

i question am i delusional or simply losing it?

losing my grip on myself or

losing my grip on reality?

but what's really real from the fallacies in a world of imitations?

in a world of falsifications?

and even more exaggerations?

as the truth so easily gets lost

what is the real cost of not knowing?

of not going forward?

of not growing anymore?

or are these all simply delusional questions of my own making?

or a result of my own unguided decision-making?

decisions that left me with sporadic emotions,

as a result of my own false devotions to things and people of this world

but my father reminded me that i am not of this world,

simply an occupant

and i can easily get lost in this world

if it is not Him i look to as my confidant

as the real illusion lies in where i reach my conclusions

for God Himself is no illusion

yet the illusion lies in my seeking elsewhere for only answers he can provide me

yet so lost was i until i decided it was simply too delusional

to continue on with the illusion i could find the answers myself

so found am i that to reach any other conclusion other than God

would be accepting the illusion i reached these conclusions myself

Misplaced loyalty...

i learned the hard way to watch where my loyalty lies
because when loyalty died
i was left with a bunch of lies disguised as truth
only to question what good is truth if no one is true?
only to question who should i be loyal to?
if lies are the new truth
and loyalty is like a removable tattoo
while love is quoted more than its given
and little difference exists between real and fiction

i was caught up the in a fictitious dimension of living
blinded by materialistic consumption
barely functioning
or accomplishing advancements
caught up in a trance
while time continued to advance without me

i lost me while
searching for acceptance
experiencing rejection
objecting my heavenly father's instructions
and cutting myself off from my own blessings

my loyalty was misplaced
and i learned i was mistaken
to think those i gave my trust to wouldn't break it
instead my loyalty was forsaken
and i was awaken to the reality of my error
that loyalty without God is empty
and i without God could only experience more emptiness
not loyalty!

Trials...

i was taught some time ago
to ask not questions of trials,
for my trials are meant to ask questions of me
as who i am and have become and one day will be
answers any unasked or asked questions any trial could ever ask of me

so the question is what do my trials say of me?
not what do i have to say of my trials
not why is it always me going through another struggle?
but what can i learn from my latest troubles?
as trials are every bit a part of me
as they are every bit a part of life
so i don't expect trials to spare me
or to spare my life

because each trial has been a test
with each victory a testimony
with each testimony
being a testament of my perseverance
for my trials speak for me
the words my actions would implore
as i continue to explore
the limits of the said impossible,
i remain a believer that all things are possible
and all trials are conquerable
when fear is conquered

for trials are mastered
only when faced head on
when fear is removed
and courage presses on

yet trials are never far away,
being very persistent
in disrupting lives
yet i was taught the strong-willed
are even more insistent
that trials are only temporary
like contemporary fashion trends
so i contend my trials are past and present
reminders of those obstacles
in life that threaten to bind me but failed
instead, i let each victory answer the questions
of my trials
while what my trials say of me is found in each victory

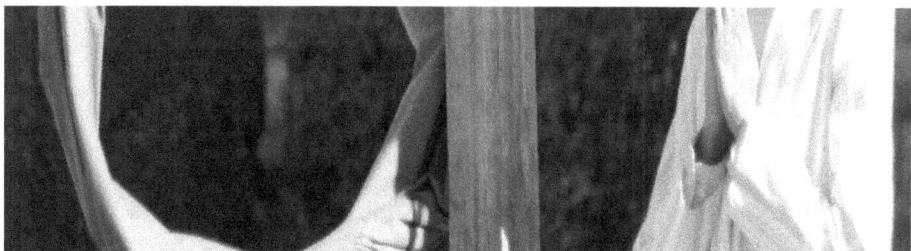

Who loves me? Why me? What is my purpose? Where am I going? Why did that happen? What is love? Is this it? Which direction do I go? Who do I turn to? Does anyone hear me? Does anyone see me? Am I changing? Have I changed? How much have I really grown? Who am I? How important is faith? What really matters? How important is love? Why don't they love me? What is the motive? What is love's purpose? What is a valid question? What is the point of curiosity? What is the purpose of learning? Why do I write? Why did I start writing? Who do I write for? What purpose do I write for? What purpose does my writing serve? What is the lesson? Does age matter? Who is God? What did the experience reveal? Is God real? Can I really be myself? How did society get here? What's perception? What is to become of tomorrow? What does the future hold? Who is going to help the kids? Why do we hate more than we love? What do I want to be? What do I want to accomplish? What will it take to get there? Is the sky my limit? What will I be remembered for? Why do I share my poetry? Who is my inspiration? What is my inspiration? Is it time to let go? How much time do I have left? What do I regret? What is the meaning of life? What is truth? How do I get to Heaven? Is love ever forever? Am I dreaming? Is this real? What is an illusion? Why am I hurting? Why do I care? Who do I admire? What is a friend? What is the meaning of family? What is fear? Am I afraid or cautious? Why do I pray? Are prayers really heard? Can I love again? How do I forgive? How do I move past the pain? Can I forgive her? Can I forgive him? What is a mother? What is a father? What is success? Where does my peace come from? Why do I smile? Can I trust her? Can I trust him? Why a book?

what is love?

Love:

attraction based on sexual desire;
affection and tenderness felt by lovers

Thanks to my first love...

i want to thank my first love for showing and giving me the love i
needed at the time
because i was lost yet feeling myself,
and needed to be found to be grounded in order to better myself
yet i was the new girl from a small town in a big city for the first time
and had never been surrounded by so many divinely fine women at one
time in my existence
which made it so easy to get caught up in all the attention i was getting
but what i noticed was the attention i wasn't getting from her

because she was indeed different
and wasn't feeling me nor the weak game i was spitting
insisting i would quit before i did all it took to have her
but i was persistent
and couldn't explain even to myself why this one was so different
but she was

she was the first to openly challenge my intentions
insisting i was a kid playing games
and working at gamestop did little to discredit her claims about me
so she ignored my persistence at first
instead she provided the first flat line to my ego
because she wasn't even feeling me at first

yet her disinterest only made my desire to have her worse
because i didn't want the thirst of women running after me anymore
i wanted the woman who would lead me
and maybe even teach me a thing or two
and i knew it had to be her
and eventually she would teach me what hadn't been taught to me
previously

by teaching me what love was
because i was a newly young adult
yet i didn't even know what love was
i didn't even know the difference between love and pain
because love and pain had always been one in the same for me

but she came from a different angle in her attempt to love me
like she was an angel sent down to make sure love didn't hurt me
and she even refused to desert me when i claimed i wasn't worthy of
the love she giving
yet she was always willing to be there
and she made me accept that she was there

and though it took some time to get me to stop running
she taught me love because she never broke her promise
she promised she'd be there as long as i allowed it
and all i had to do was value her love & never want to go without it

and for as long as it was meant to last i never wanted to be without her
love
even when we thought our moment had passed us
love would again out last us
and refuse to let the past be us

but when the past became us
neither of us was the same us
because she had made a young kid grow up
and corrected the distorted image in my head i had of love
from growing up where love and pain was one in the same
instead her love provided a change i was in need of
and i would never be the same after the love she gave me
because in some regards it was her love that saved me
when i was being more than a little reckless

until her love overwhelmed me and let me breathless
left me redirecting the ill-advised moves i was making
to embrace a love that was mine for the taken
without fear that love would take my heart and break it

instead i experienced the power of love for the first time
and i was provided with just the right amount of love i needed
so this piece is to thank my first love for teaching me how to concede to love
for teaching me how to receive your love
because without the lesson i would have never learned how to adjust to love
i would have never learned just how powerful love can be
but most of all, i would have never experienced the feeling of you loving me

"I dedicate **'Thanks to my first love...'** to the woman who taught me how to love, the beautiful Taneshia Harris. I want to thank you from the depths of me for giving me the love I needed at the time and for continuing to give me the love of a true friend years past our last shared kiss. I love you and I always will. ~Indy

Love will happen...

so many of us wonder why "the one" we thought were "the one" turned out to be "the one" who hurt us more than "the one" before.

and no matter how badly we wanted "the one" to work out, we eventually realized "the one" was not "the one" just like before.

so many of us become afraid that maybe we'll never find "the one" that will capture our mind, soul, and heart unlike "the one" before.

afraid we will live forever alone without finding "the one" that cares more, gives more, loves more unlike "the one" before.

and we become so tired of not finding "the one" that we begin a desperate search at finding "the one" really meant for us unlike "the one" before and make the greatest mistake in doing so.

because nothing good usually comes out of desperation and it's likely we end up with someone worse than "the one" before them.

only to question why does this one not love me just like "the one" before them.

i ask myself these same questions each time another chapter closes and the mingling comes and goes

but i haven't found the answers yet and only part of the solution but i did discover:

love finds us just when we stop looking for love and start looking for fun.

love finds us when we leave our heart open and allow God's work to be done.

so i'm no longer looking for love but looking for fun and trusting love will happen on its own.

sidenote: (i'm not in love, but i sure am having fun.)

Music and its lyrics...

your entry into my life

has been like an out of body experience

soothing my troubled soul of late

comforting me in times of sadness

slipping over and under the very walls i try to hide behind

as the music and its lyrics reveal those pieces of me i've tried to conceal the most

and the melodies expose me

unclothing me and leaving me naked

baring my objections,

past rejections,

and the directions i once followed that got me lost

before your entry

i was one lost cause waiting for something

i didn't know what that something was

but i could feel the vibrations of each note

as it echoed inside my hollow hole

a hole now filling slowly

half full rather than empty

as your entry into my life

has awakened me

the music elevates my soul

and the lyrics uplift me

to a height ecstasy couldn't take me

so i now submit to the music

and commit to the lyrics wholeheartedly

i submit to my release

from self-inflicted captivity

i submit to breath

to feel, to live

through the music and its lyrics.

Tripping...

this distance obviously has me tripping

because it's only been a day

yet it's no way I can go on pretending

like it doesn't matter when you are out my sight

because truth is you are the light that brightens my day

and nothing seems to go right when you're not a part of it

it's like my chest has no heart in it

because something is obviously missing

when I experience this distance

and everything I try to do is met with resistance

though I'm not sure it was your intention

but you take "missing you" to a new dimension

because be assured you are my only one

and I be straight tripping when you don't come around me

only because I sometimes get confused

and forget you not my wife...yet

but if I could I would fast forward time in jet speed

just to make you the lady forever next to me

never too proud to plead my case

because just in case you forgot

it only took the first look upon your angelic face

before I was jumping up to fix your plate

and prepared to wait however long it would take

for the right time I could share these thoughts of mine

yet lucky for me I obviously left some kind of good impression

because you didn't turn down my suggestion that we kick it

and I been blessed by your presence ever since

blessed by the presence of God that resides in you

now I thank God daily for taking His time on you

and I thank you both for the time I spend with you

yet I'd be lying if I omitted the obvious

I'd probably spend all my time with you
which is probably why a day away is a day times two
yet I'm obviously tripping
because it really has only been one day
yet this is how it be when I'm away from you
straight tripping
even when I only spend a day away from you

Wishing well...

i was a wishing well
wishing time would remove my shell
and allow me to prevail in her world
because she was the girl i hoped for
and continuously wished for

until one day i finally received what i wished for
and she was all that i hoped for
so i became our wishing well
wishing us well
wishing our love never fails
wishing for a love that always prevails
and propels genuine happiness

yet all my wishing was for no avail
because our love did indeed fail us over time
now all i have is wishes to replace the kisses we once shared
wishes to remind me of an us that i'm now missing
and wishes to counter the nightmares of our failure

so now i must wish you one last farewell
as i mourn for a love that no longer prevails
as i mourn for an us that no longer exists
despite the persistence of my many wishes
so i wish you a permanent farewell
with one last wish i ask of you
that you never forget that our love could have never existed without the
persistence of my very first wish to have you...

Inevitable...

this heart ache i'm feeling was avoidable yet inevitable
because i ignored the warning signs screaming
"be careful with your heart, play your part,
and be smart about it"
but i was once again hardheaded
now it's my heart that's harden
wanting to forgot how we started
and even more the reasons behind why we parted
because i'm feeling the consequences
of leaving my heart unguarded again

yet i admit i was intentionally blind sometimes
to the truth in front of me
seeing only that i wanted to see
intentionally not hearing your lies
wanting so badly to believe you
even in moments when you couldn't meet my eyes
even in moments i knew your truth to be a lie
yet despite knowing better
i chose lesser for myself
so caught up in the moment was i
i forgot we were simply sharing moments
no expectations or empty promises?

but i was everything but smart about it
playing a bigger part than i should have
left only with empty hopes of what could have been
because you called it quits
not ready for a relationship
and while that should have been the end of it
i wanted to believe the inevitable wasn't imminent

only feelings proved more complicated
when your departure came about unexpectantly
and without much of an explanation
that you didn't owe me
yet knowing and going through it
proved to be harder to stomach
and just move on from than the circumstances warranted

even knowing what was coming
couldn't prepare me for the inevitable
because this heart ache im feeling
is because i ignored the warning signs screaming
be careful, play your part, & be smart about it

Write about you...

once again i've wasted some of my better lines
on what turned out to be
nothing more than a good time
as i openly revealed emotions you were evoking
i manipulated real feelings into spoken words
feeling my heart and mind had finally chosen
the girl who was most deserving of me
and eventually the gate to my emotions was opened
as feelings flowed from inside of me
i allowed my poetry to confide for me
the beauty in you sharing priceless moments with me
now i find myself choking back the very tears
i most feared that were always nearby
crying the same type of tears
you promised i would never cry
facing an end i was promised would never come
yet now that it's all said and done
i realize never is an insincere time to promise anyone
because i discovered it's not our wants
that keep the inevitable from coming
now i'm left rereading the very lines
written just for you
the supposedly permanent boo
that turned a good half in two
temporarily
now i'm writing some of my best lines
about the inconvenient truth
of how loving all of you
couldn't ensure the promise
you would love me too
as your sincerity wasn't well-perceived by me

because you turned out to be
everything you declared not to be
a parody of your so-called truth
while the inconvenient truth is
i'm still writing some of my best lines
about you but without you

Love Lost its way...

when i see old married couples
celebrating anniversaries
i see a love that hasn't changed
and has withstood the tests of time
a love that's been blessed
and now respected
by those like myself who simply want to know their secret

because nowadays love seems to have lost its way
and people don't love like they did in the old days
back when if a heart was broken
it was fixed, not thrown away
back when love held firm
and didn't stray away
back when kisses
were saved for a first date
and homeruns were saved for a later date

old married couples simply say
love not for quitters
because back in the good old days
lovers tried talking it out
before they walked out on each other
because love was about accepting all the faults
and not quickly discarding the heart when things weren't going right

the simple things still counted and spoke what the heart couldn't
verbally say
simple things like love letters were still written and saved as forbidden
secrets
a dating period predated intimacy

nowadays it's just easier to be intimate
because love is not a requirement to being intimate
like in the old days when love was the motive
and lovers were devoted to each other
through sickness and health
for richer or poorer
for better or worse

but nowadays it seems love has lost its way
because nobody loving like they did back in the old days
back when if love wasn't loving you long
then love was loving you wrong

Possibilities...

those in love encourage me not to ignore the possibilities of love
but i'm asking myself after experiencing love
how do i now embrace the possibilities of love again?
because my pastimes have only had hostility to offer me
each time feeling the rejection of myself without conditions
each time receiving contradictory conditions in return
despite the loving disposition i'm consistently giving
those fairy tale fictions aren't being duplicated
nor is the effort i'm giving being replicated
now all those thoughts of possibility just seem outdated to me
because they also predated the last possibility
when i was all caught up in our complimenting chemistry
and my heart was informing me
it was ready to transform me
fortunately for me, before the transformation was complete
the truth put the dust back under my feet
just as quickly as she swept me up in her deceit
now my mental remains judgmental of these possibilities
that could very much be detrimental to the little i have left
because i don't know if i can give another soul my all without the bias
and seriously trust my heart won't die if i try again
that love won't make me cry again
but then again
i ask of myself how can i deny the possibilities of love
if i don't embrace the opportunities of love
and still say with a straight face
that love is simply a waste of time if i don't give it my time
yet i ask of those in love who believe love to be so divine
how can i replace this distaste of mind
if my heart is blocking any attempts at it being replaced
how can i allow another to trace the path to my heart again

if my heart is refusing to embrace the possibilities of love again?

how can i go from loving a friend

to falling in love with my best friend

if my heart is so focused on the inevitable end

tell me how can i embrace the possibilities of love

and assure my heart i won't experience

the deficiencies hidden in the very same opportunities those in love say
i should try again?

Love on purpose...

there was once upon a time
i wanted to fall in love on purpose
and i was convinced that love should be the motive
and it was worth it even if it hurt a little bit
so i got my bits and pieces of love
yet love left me in a million pieces
and when once i thirst for love
like a street feign with an addiction
my heart is now guarded
and comes with more provisions
than entrances

so though i notice that you're different
than what i'm used to
all those other girls before you were different once too
saying everything i wanted to hear
doing everything i needed
until the little things became the things that were missing
and kissing sessions were replaced with arguments

so no, i'm not in a rush to feel the eruption of my heart again
and fall into the trap again of believing pretty girls don't lie
because they do
so i long ago concluded
most females are one in the same
with different names,
but always the same games
making the same claims with the same aims
way beyond the range of my patience

then there is you offering something supposedly different

insisting exceptions still exist
of exceptional love
that love can still be something worth fighting for if i'm not fighting alone
but i have been fighting alone too many times to remember
back when i still wanted to fall in love on purpose
yet each heartbreak has convinced me more
that maybe love just isn't worth all this hurting
even more now i'm suspicious of intentions
because no one ever mentions
how limited their love is in the beginning
only later realizing i'd been used for the benefits

yet here you are still
despite my trust issues
and stubborn refusal
to see you without suspicions
insisting you're different than those before you
and though you're tempting me
i don't know if i could
i don't know if i can do it again
another heartbreak could prove fatal
and i just don't know if i'm able to come back from another near death experience

when not long ago i wanted to fall in love on purpose
when nothing inhibited my heart
and i still saw love without bias
when i still believed love could leave one breathless
and be a priceless, timeless
creation of art
to be treasured for years and years

and i don't know if that's what you're offering me
but it's the only thing i'm accepting
because lowered expectations
left only me as the one experiencing the neglect
now all i have is a heart full of reflections
so i hope you can understand why i'm second-guessing
and expressing so much doubt
it's just that love hasn't been what i read about
yet i'm still convinced it could be just like what i read about

despite the times love didn't work out for me
or maybe it was the girls that just wasn't right for me
because love didn't hurt me,
it was the person i chose to love who hurt me
and despite my negativity on the topic
i find myself drifting back to those moments before the pain, the lies,
the shame, & the end game
still believing love to be worth all that comes with it
still a hopeless romantic still believing not all love people give treats you
the same
and the ending can change or never come

truth is, part of me still desires to fall in love on purpose
and though i'm not feeling love is worth all the hurting i been through
i'm willing to leave my hurt open and hope love is true this time
i'm hoping you're real this time
and not just spitting lines to get my attention
because we can still be friends without the benefits

yet you say you're here because you believe love can be infinite
that love is worth it and it doesn't have to hurt me
nor will all love desert me
because you've felt what i'm now feeling

and though it took you a minute
to get over the pain
you acknowledge it is the stain love left behind
that reminds you that love can only be beautiful
when two hearts both agree to fall in love on purpose
and you now desire to fall in love on purpose with me

Beautiful stranger...

i was approached by a beautiful stranger one night
and it felt as if we had previously met
but she did not know me
and i did not know her
yet i still felt like i knew her
for her vibes felt so familiar to me
with a body made for worshipping
and beauty not easily forgotten
then i would remember
that she perfectly mirrored the lady i often dream about
with the perfect smile situated between deep dimples
and captivating eyes that lure you in without your permission
and then she spoke to me
whispering she has been waiting for me
awaiting the day when she could depart my dream
and fill the empty space within me
but then she begin to slip away from me
dissolving into the air
whispering she still waits for me
as the sun hit my face
awakening me to the reality
that the beautiful stranger
still remains the lady i often dream about

Anonymous...

you and i share an anonymous love that currently goes unspoken

as we've been chosen to love in a time yet to exist

unknowingly awaiting a time when a first kiss will seal our fates

because despite our impatience with waiting time is not being wasted on us

time is simply providing experience to better prepare us for a love like we've never experienced

a love we long ago desired before love lost its innocence

and our outlook on love hasn't been the same ever since love stop making sense to us

because love hasn't been very patient nor kind to us,

leaving us both envious from time to time of a love others boast about

but love isn't supposed to be boastful nor proud

nor should love dishonor others or be self-seeking

instead, love should be slow to anger with no record of who did what wrong or the reason

with no delight found in the evil that stripped trust from us

because love itself is to be rejoiced where there is happiness and trust in us

protecting us and trusting us,

always hoping and persevering

never to fail us

but up until now our efforts to give love have failed us

and our hearts have been temporarily derailed

though God is using this time to repair us

to be made anew just for us to trust the situations our hearts have been through were all for this purpose

that all those heart breaks and heart aches were worth it

and all the things we had to go through to grow through

was preparing us for a moment we've been promised

for our destiny connects us
because God has preselected us
you for me and i for you
but only when our hearts are ready for each other
after we've grown enough to know how to appreciate one another
to cherish a love perfectly created to be treasured forever between us
in the meantime we continue to wait
while in between times we both grow in our faith
for the purpose of learning how to rightfully love you and you love me
though for now our love remains anonymous
a love synonymous with the love God has promised us

Anticipating...

anticipating what is to come

has me about to cum

before i even hear you moan

and if this feeling is wrong

then i disown what's right

knowing nothing could suffice

such an immaculate sight

and i can't wait to see you naked

with nipples erected just for me

like they inviting me

to tease then feast on your perfection

with so many times previously

i made love to you in my mind

i undressed you without touching you,

lusting for you

though an imagination of anticipation

does no justice for you

for i'm ready to explore your body

like it's my favorite hobby

with plans tailored to skip the romance

in anticipation of travel

from the top until i work my way down

downtown that is

where your jewel is

placing kisses,

leaving hickeys,

yet slowly because i don't do quickies

i insist on you letting me tie up your wrists

so you can't resist this lick down

i'm about to put down on you

with promises to have all kinds

of sounds coming out of you

because i'm on a personal mission to challenge

every possible position you ever envisioned your body in

with the only intermission being

for your secretion to flow into my mouth

as i feed down south so my apologies in advance

for the jealousy of other extremities

but me and your clitoris

have a special chemistry that creates

the sweetest of melodies for my sexual therapy

with my intentions to climax you mentally

and send your body into ecstasy..

as the devotee to your pleasantry

and my tongue weaponry

that goes steadily

until your entire body is shaking warily

then you will be begging me to stop

but i won't until the arc in your back finally drops..

and i can feel the vibrancy

of your body weakening beneath me

with your juices feeding me

with the seasoning of your sweetness

and hear your body speaking

of the max peaking of your climax

as i embody you close to me

already anticipating

when i can give you another dose of me

Who loves me? Why me? What is my purpose? Where am I going? Why did that happen? What is love? Is this it? Which direction do I go? Who do I turn to? Does anyone hear me? Does anyone see me? Am I changing? Have I changed? How much have I really grown? Who am I? How important is faith? What really matters? How important is love? Why don't they love me? What is the motive? What is love's purpose? What is a valid question? What is the point of curiosity? What is the purpose of learning? Why do I write? Why did I start writing? Who do I write for? What purpose do I write for? What purpose does my writing serve? What is the lesson? Does age matter? Who is God? What did the experience reveal? Is God real? Can I really be myself? How did society get here? What is perception? What is to become of tomorrow? What does the future hold? Who is going to help the kids? Why do we hate more than we love? What do I want to be? What do I want to accomplish? What will it take to get there? Is the sky my limit? What will I be remembered for? Why do I share my poetry? Who is my inspiration? What is my inspiration? Is it time to let go? How much time do I have left? What do I regret?

What is the meaning of life? What is truth? How do I get to Heaven? Is love ever forever? Am I dreaming? Is this real? What is an illusion? Why am I hurting? Why do I care? Who do I admire? What is a friend? What is the meaning of family? What is fear? Am I afraid or cautious? Why do I pray? Are prayers really heard? Can I love again? How do I forgive? How do I move past the pain? Can I forgive her? Can I forgive him? What is a mother? What is a father? What is success? Where does my peace come from? Why do I smile? Can I trust her? Can I trust him? Why a book?

Why do I write?

write:

To express or communicate in
writing; give a written account of

Respect my mic...

i politely ask that you respect my mic
because i'm a poet
and not a rapper
this is not hip hop you can pop to
but poetry meant to shock you awake
the beat you don't hear is not more important than my verses
and my meaning is more than what you do hear on the surface
a meaning that's no good to you if you don't hear the beginning
with an ending that has no purpose
if you miss the purpose behind why i'm spitting in the first place

because i'm not freestyle spitting
but spitting about real issues,
real living
and how to put a stop to
the glorified killings
and the street dealing
and how to motivate more of
independent thinkers
and entrepreneurs
and have less of
poverty stricken school children with no chance to grow up
and able bodied adults who keep failing to show up
in a society where the news gives murderers a close up
and victims are easily forgotten like back page news stories

but i'm not your local five o'clock news story
so i politely ask you to respect my mic
so i can give you a different point of view
you're not accustomed to hearing
and inspire you to become conscious of your way of living

but at the very least i hope my words inspire you to
talk more,
listen more,
do more,
be more
because this world needs more

more love and less drugs
more lyrics and less beat
more people practicing what they preach
and more people willing to speak out
and not turn a deaf ear to people like me

me...
a poet and not a rapper
with spoken words as my chosen words
and not just the best rhyming word to finish a sequence of sentences
with an emphasis on the message
that remains hidden until it's processed
because there can be no progress before the process of enlightenment
and new heights can't be reach if thinking isn't heightened
beyond in the box thinking

so i protest your refusal to turn off your soap box for a minute and listen
to me
to give me your attention
and stop resisting what's different than what you're used to hearing
because we've suddenly gotten used to less substance and more
corruptive media
now we have more violent eruptions
with less loving and no solutions

but rather than doing nothing

i offer my contributions through spitting
and ask for your respect for why i do this
understand there is no blueprint to follow
and my words remain hollow if not injected

so i politely ask you to respect my mic
because i'm a poet, not a rapper
not offering answers,
but questioning the standards we all live by...

Silent emotions...

what is to be thought of my emotions that go unheard, never to be spoken of?

do they not deserve the right to exist?

for whose right is it to resist

my expression, my confessions

for whose right is it to decide

the relevancy my life lessons consist of

for whose right is it to protest how i channel my emotions

for whose right is it to instruct how i heal from my own brokenness

from my incomplete changes,

from inappropriate exchanges,

from the times previously i allowed silence to chain me

even more so whose right is it to tell me the emotions i can & cannot speak of

for my silence only voids the story behind both my visible & hidden scars

for my silence suggests what i have to say is irrelevant

for my silence implies my emotions have no meaning

and yet my silence only silences me

therefore, is not silence the cowardly decision to make?

as if i've been sanctioned to speak only when invited

implying i need permission to release of me

to give of me the flowing stream of my emotions

because baseless become the emotions silence prohibits the world's ears from hearing

baseless are the emotions my silence keeps me from sharing

baseless are the emotions silence prevents the world from comprehending

from feeling

from extending their understanding of my struggles

of my troubles

of the obstacles that almost made it impossible at times for me to press forward

because for so long my emotions were everything but straightforward truth

yet i was soothed by the inconvenient truth that silent emotions cannot speak

they are neither heard or discerned as long as they are silent

as long as they remain caged emotions seen only through my violent tendencies

while privately a riot wages inside of me

preventing me from achieving the freedom to just be one with my peace

yet if my emotions could speak would anyone listen?

would anyone insist that i continue spitting

simply because they can relate to me,

or fully understand the daily challenges facing me

as i seek to end my silence

to replace the violence of my past

with words that last beyond the pain

and perfectly frame my emotions

i now seek to disassociate myself with the emotionally silent

coming full circle my emotions are now empowered

as i have discovered that it is the flow of my poetry

that accurately depicts the parody of my emotions

for if nothing else,

i am a gifted writer and of no good use if my emotions remain silent

iSpit...

i spit to transition my complexity to your simplicity
giving definitions to state of affairs undefined
see this is far more than rhyming for me
it's capturing time and giving my life meaning
beyond the invisible lines
my eyes can't see
and my brain too cloudy to make sense of
so i spit it out despite the spike in my veins
from the drain and strain of explaining it all

see i spit to draw attention
to the news not mentioned
to strengthen the hushed voices
and bring awareness to injustice
whether it be a complete stranger
or my own misfortune

i spit because i see life different
for knowledge is the key for the ignorant
and though definitions remain unknown
atonement must be the desire
if we all aspire to inspire progression

i spit because silence is regression
and it's what we fail to say
that delays the good
later to highlight the shoulds
when it becomes too late
and we left with i could have

i spit to release the beast

living inside of me
covered in my afflictions
from my persistence to thrive
i spit to survive
the abuses that was all too common
by the age of five

i spit to pull an ear to my diction
when no one listens
when no one insists
nor persists when an
another kid resists...
learning!

though i'm just one girl spitting
persistently insisting knowledge be a given
it's merely a vision
when the decision is to drop out
because it's easier to cop out

though i'm just one girl spitting
to voice my diction
speaking of a vision
insisting with persistence people simply listen
i spit because its the toxin
to negate the option of quitting

Words to inspire...

i was born with words to inspire the masses.

yet i harnessed my gift back in the classrooms

where i gained knowledge assets

in preparation for problems there was no test for

yet from history to literature i learned of stories where more was accomplished

only by those with the strongest will

i learned from the story of Malcolm X that differences in opinion can and will get you killed by your brothers

yet Dr. King stayed true to his dream that i would one day be seen as an equal

while Maya Angelou still teaches of rising up and picking up the pieces

a sign of sorts that nothing great would come easy

because before i knew how far writing would lead me

it was the words of others that reached me

now i'm committed to spitting because it is the gift that fuels me

and allows me to make sense of all the confusion that surrounds me

so even if this world ignores my whispers

this world cannot ignore my screams

because i will no longer be silent

my words are defiant of any attempts of verbal confinement

as the first amendment gives me the freedom to say fuck being compliant

so i commit myself to spitting my truth without contentment

and no resentment for the experiences that often leave me short-winded

i defend my right to be independent in my thinking

with words to inspire the main stream

as my purpose is more than a mere daydream

because i dream of something much bigger than myself

not measured by wealth

nor by my social network friend count

instead i dream of a mass awakening of defeated spirits

of inspiring those who appear lost in a mental wilderness

of reaching those who have dreams but face limits

of walking in the footsteps of those whose words inspire me

like the words of Langston Hughes that encourage me to hold fast to my dreams

unless i wish to be grounded like a wingless bird

with words that cannot inspire anyone

for i am bound to a purpose of uplifting others

with words that allow me to reach out through my documented struggles

and serve as lessons learned from my troubles

for my silence is a disservice of my worth to this world

and i would do more harm to this world if i was to conform to this world

yet i choose to follow the words of leaders

by using words to explore myself and life deeper

because experience has been my best teacher

and my words make each lesson clearer

as i aspire to use words to inspire many before my own time expires

I want my poetry to...

i want my poetry to reveal the ills that fill me

of heavy pressure,

brutal measures,

night terrors,

and bad scenes that weren't dreams but my reality

i want my poetry to portray my actuality as your fiction

and your calm as my friction

to mimic the constant tension i've lived with

i want my poetry to cry for me without tears

for the years of fearing verbal, physical, & sexual abuse

i want my poetry to wrap warmness around the cold shoulders

who turned their backs when my life had no track at all

i want my poetry to speak my silence when my voice was powerless

further weakened by my cowardice choice to remain silent

i want my poetry to teach others the lessons i've learned

from constant tragedies amongst countless casualties

i want my poetry to evoke emotions

that spark connections of my past reflections

i want my poetry to mirror my mental,

transcribe my thoughts,

and voice the passions that lie within my heart

i want my poetry to talk my talk

and walk my walk for me

whispering my secrets,

telling my history,

yelling my insecurities,

and demanding attention of others to just listen or read

as my poetry speaks of the conditions i've lived with, lived thru & still living

i want my poetry to tell of me

the joys,

the trials,

the passions,

the heartache,

the heart breaks

moreover, i want my poetry to give me the outlet i need

when voiced words aren't always choice words

and bad words aren't always nice words

while written words, whether spoken or never verbally expressed,

are powerful nonetheless

Writer's block...

there are moments faced in life

where there are more questions than answers

more problems than solutions

and times where there is nothing to explain

the roots of it all

yet as a writer you put pen to paper

only to hit wall after wall

producing nothing more than meaningless rambles

yet needing badly a release

instead each line written seems to reflect

and more so deflect present feelings to the next day

while hope is simply for tomorrow

to be better, not bitter

and yesterday not be some predictor

of things to come.

yet tomorrow comes

and yesterday stubbornly remains

as the blank page reflects the same

blank space it was yesterday

and yesterday's problems

are now today's bothers

and potentially tomorrow's worries

as words appear to have abandoned you,

and the weight of unreleased emotions

threaten to overwhelm you

the unintentional silence has the potential

to disrupt a many thoughts

and bring about even more sleepless nights

nights when blank pages remain blank spaces

and a writers worse nightmare consumes reality

when memories remain wasted energies

and tragedies remain unwritten masterpieces
when blockage holds hostage the deepest of confessions
and threatens inescapable bondage
when unreleased emotions threaten to suffocate
with each thought that goes unwritten
a reminder of lingering emotions that strangle you
for a writer has little reason left to breathe
if there are no words to be written
if there are no final chapters or solid conclusions
one is left with only illusions
while internally problems continue to brew
until pent up frustrations
eventually boil over
in an inappropriate display of emotions
for to take a writer's words away
is like a lethal injection
slowly paralyzing all abilities to properly function
this is why to take a writer's words away
is the worse possible form of punishment

Not done yet...

i've reached the end of another piece

to still find myself without peace

because i'm not done yet

as a single thought transcends several pages

my mind wages war

against the emotions exploding within me

while my own self-doubt threatens to inhibit me

and fails to accurately depict me

instead picture me as an incomplete puzzle

with scattered pieces

as a pre-mature fetus

still learning to breathe

as a lost about sinner

knocked down to my knees

praying to my God to hear my pleas

once was lost but found when i confessed

as i end another piece to share my expression

i still find myself without peace

because i'm not done yet

like an incomplete press release

with missing details

a hard to sale story

when there is so much more to speak about

so much more i see

that i don't read about

so much more i don't hear

because society prefers to simply forget about it.

yet i can't ignore the brokenness i'm feeling

nor the toll this straining is draining from me

as i strain to cling to the last bit of authenticity

i explore the depths of subliminal messages

that redirect the meaning of the message
and gets lost among a page full of words
that collectively make-up another piece
only to find i've reached the end of another piece
to still find myself without peace
because i'm not done yet

Who loves me? Why me? What is my purpose? Where am I going? Why did that happen? What is love? Is this it? Which direction do I go? Who do I turn to? Does anyone hear me? Does anyone see me? Am I changing? Have I changed? How much have I really grown? Who am I? How important is faith? What really matters? How important is love? Why don't they love me? What is the motive? What is love's purpose? What is a valid question? What is the point of curiosity? What is the purpose of learning? Why do I write? Why did I start writing? Who do I write for? What purpose do I write for? What purpose does my writing serve? What is the lesson? Does age matter? Who is God? What did the experience reveal? Is God real? Can I really be myself? How did I get here? What is perception? What is to become of tomorrow? What does the future hold? Who is going to help the kids? Why do we hate more than we love? What do I want to be? What do I want to accomplish? What will it take to get there? Is the sky my limit? What will I be remembered for? Why do I share my poetry? Who is my inspiration? What is my inspiration? Is it time to let go? How much time do I have left? What do I regret? What is the meaning of life? What is truth? How do I get to Heaven? Is love ever forever? Am I dreaming? Is this real? What is an illusion? Why am I hurting? Why do I care? Who do I admire? What is a friend? What is the meaning of family? What is fear? Am I afraid or cautious? Why do I pray? Are prayers really heard? Can I love again? How do I forgive? How do I move past the pain? Can I forgive her? Can I forgive him? What is a mother? What is a father? What is success? Where does my peace come from? Why do I smile? Can I trust her? Can I trust him? Why a book?

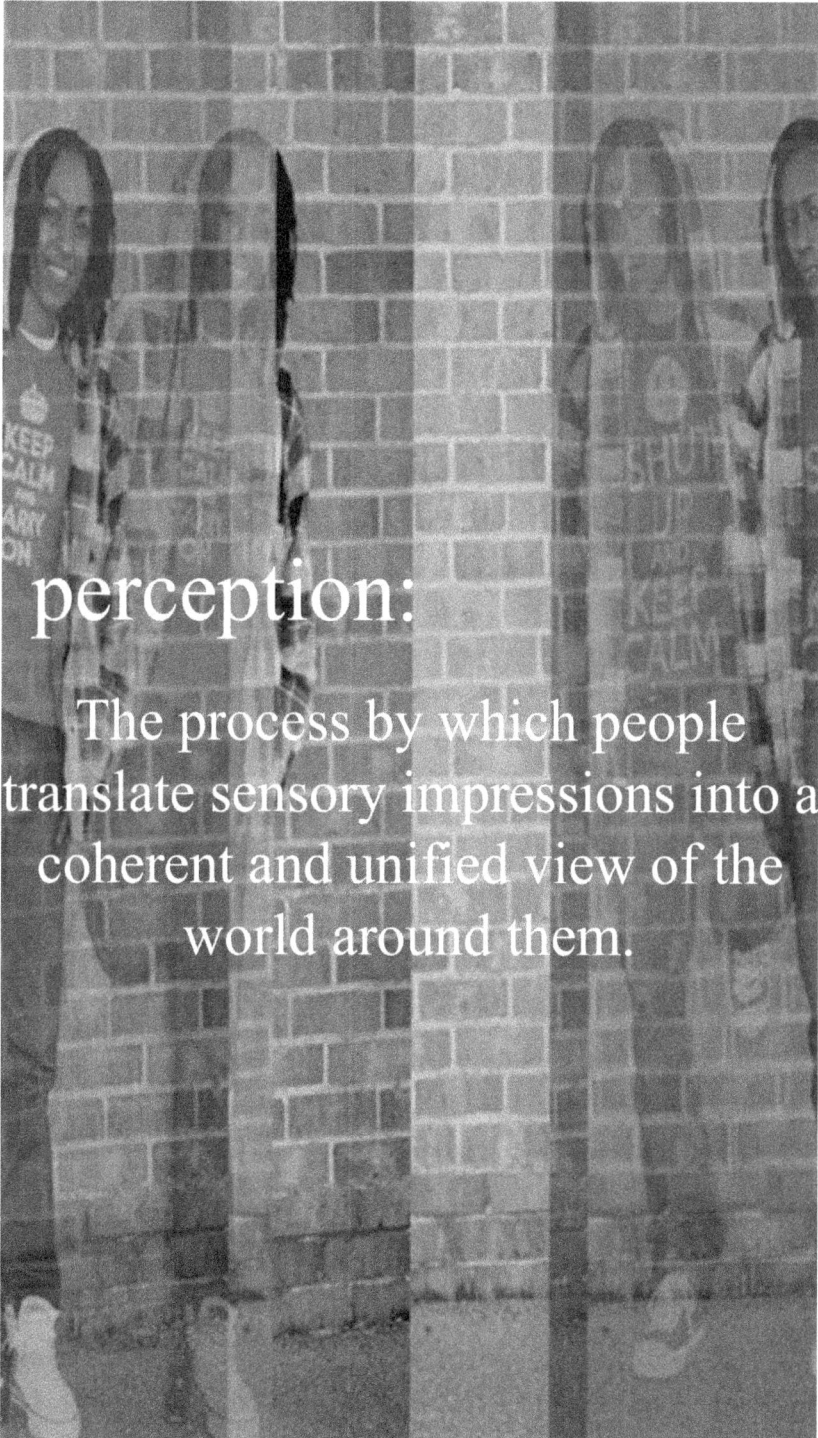

perception:

The process by which people translate sensory impressions into a coherent and unified view of the world around them.

Definition of beauty...

hey there beautiful, yes you

i want to encourage you to stop searching for beauty

and desiring change of yourself in the name of beauty

but know you are the beauty in the word beautiful

you are the standard to the answer of how you define beauty

the natural depiction of beauty's very own dictionary definition

the perfect calm to what's ugly about friction in this world

the perfect verse to decrease what's ugly about tension in this world

yet to conclude anything else about yourself would be entirely fiction

because i'm certain you are mother nature's best decision yet

so glow in your birthday suit which is your natural suit

and try modeling the all-natural look without the deceptive shield of cosmetic makeup

because all that makeup does is serve as a disguise

while that mascara conceals the natural twinkle of your eyes

yet your search for beauty & desire to change hides the beauty that is you

tho i can't say i'd call you beautiful if you went changing things

in an attempt to rearrange the very things about you that make you beautiful

so close those magazines

and stop with the comparisons

and start ignoring what these image consultants are selling

before you sell yourself out

becoming someone you once knew

that you thought should be you

but understand it would no longer be you

because beauty requires being true to the person in the mirror staring back at you

yet you're insisting on add-ons

when i'm already turned on by what i see, by what i hear, by i feel when i'm near you and i cheer for the beauty pouring out from inside of you

that gives the final resolution to the definition of your beauty

for it's not simply a pictorial representation that defines your beauty,

but it's the pieces of you on the inside combined with the outside that define your beauty

so i'm inclined to encourage you to stop searching for beauty..

and desiring change in the name of beauty

but know you are the beauty in the world beautiful

Crushing...

i'm way too grown to be crushing like a school girl
but there i was, afraid to talk to that girl

out of fear she didn't even like girls
but not brave enough to ask

so i admired her in passing
always wanting the moment to last a little longer than the last one

yet next time came and went
and she just walked pass me

and i blew another chance to at least say hello
so maybe next time she notices me

but my voice seems to abandon me whenever she's in my vicinity
and her very presence seems to knock the wind out of me

leaving me feeling butterflies and seeing fire flies
all for this girl who doesn't even know i'm alive

this girl who makes me feel tingly inside with just a flash of her smile

a smile i only see every once in a while
because she's just a crush i'm crushing on
because despite being way too grown for this
i'm crushing like a school girl, afraid to talk to that girl...

now i than wrote about her and i don't even know her name...

Impression...

for i've been impressed by you
left with permanent impressions of you
left with markings like permanent etchings of you
carved in my mental since our very first encounter
the experience itself has been like a surreal obsession
and i find myself breathless, overwhelmed by your impression

for i have been impressed by you
captivated by the permanent impressions left by you
the experience itself has been an impression of you
that reminds me of your impression on me

for i confess my transgression
is wanting another moment
another time or event
to share with you
or simply exist in with you

for i've been impressed by you
left with an impression of you
that is not enough of you
therefore i desire more of you
because a memory could never serve you in entirety
and i don't want a variety of you
i simply want you

for i've been impressed by you
left with only these permanent impressions of you
left cherishing the etchings of the impression that is you.

Mourning love...

my heart is unbearably heavy right now

as another news story broke today and i learned another fool with a gun decided innocent lives were his for the taken

now another city is shaken and the heart of our entire nation is collectively broken

in our individual homes we're hugging and pulling each other close

choking back our tears as we're all feeling a parent's biggest worry

sending our kids out into the world and the world never sending our kids back home

because each day the streets seem to get rougher

and every day another lost soul picks up a gun to prove toughness

now another mother is crying over what she didn't get a chance to say

and society is looking for which way to point the finger

and one evil act after another fills heart after heart with more hate

yet no one has the answer to the question of how we got to this state of senseless killing

instead the focus is on how much gun laws should be stricken

but we must first change ourselves and how we living

because love is missing and we all feeling it

each time a mass murder claims innocent victims

each time a school shooting claims innocent children

each time a domestic violence spat claims

another mother and another child is left alone

with no answers, it all seems so senseless

leaves even the biggest talkers speechless

searching for words to comfort ourselves and each other

we want an explanation

but innocent killing is sometimes unexplainable

and we can vote to change the laws
but we have to put the focus back on how we feeling
how we raising our children
and how we got here in the first place

because while everyone is so caught up in the blame game tomorrow
still not coming for far too many
and dreams are being cut out or cut off for far too many
and far too many are innocent victims of others evil decisions

evil only combatted if we just love each other
look to every man and woman as your sister and brother
it shouldn't matter the color
or how different their struggles are from your own
we're all a family in the this country we call our home
and if we can't love each other more than we hate each other
we'll continue to mourn more innocent victims

99%

if America is the land of opportunity
i'm asking, "where is my milk and honey?"
where is this "opportunity" we've all been promised?
because after years of blood stained sweat
from struggle and oppression
and constant rejections
since being taken from our lands
and being counted as an individual
since our inclusion in the great american constitution
we supposedly have freedom

yet freedom is oppressive in measure
because no restitution was given
no opportunity was given for independent living
so to the slums 99% of us went with our opportunity
while the 1% opened up the ghettos where we bunched together
to depend on each other to move forward with our given "opportunity"

and though opportunity was given
it was taken from our grasp due to hidden agendas
of superior figures in history elected as the people's politicians
yet to this day their true intentions remain a mystery
no different than the present state of our nation
america the great, founded on but separated by creed
consequently undone by a lack of common decency
because we're more committed to overseas expenditures
than those begging at the government's feet
for nothing more than a job
a place to make ends meet independently
all seeking the opportunity to survive
all seeking a fair chance to thrive

from a government than cares more about money than innocent lives
now present day got us repeating history
but it's even more of us living in misery because of the direct action of rich politicians

now we picketing in times square demanding a change
because a change must come
or sooner or later the 99% of us will be undone
the dreams of our daughters and sons struck down
before they leave playground school age
and present day begins to reflect the old days
with a twist
because it's no longer just African-Americans in this struggle
black, white, poor, middle class
we all united in this struggle

99% of us at least
while 1% is the majority
looking down on the minority
wallowing just above and below the poverty line
while they doing just fine in their big houses with their fancy wine
while 99% of us out here on this daily grind
with more working hours than leisure time
while the 1% got more vacation time than all of us combined
and they call it equal
but equal opportunity is nothing more than a fancy phrase used in their political speeches
because politicians rarely practice what they preach to get elected
because as soon as election is over
they give 99% of us the cold shoulder
and do more for the very 1% we all fighting against.

The blame game...

this blame game got too many talking
and nobody really walking anywhere
speaking about the way things are
and the way things have always been
that's more or less unproductive chatter
yet the main topic of daily neighborhood discussions
as many are quick to discuss the shit that don't matter
with no one in a rush to change anymore
instead too many are settling for less
afraid of the success that comes from trying
now i detest more and more this state of stagnation
that's captured too many,
too early the great minds of tomorrow's nation
too many of the great minds that will never come to fruition
too many of the great minds caught up in enslavement
like they waiting for master to give them permission
but slavery's over and no one needs permission to change
or to break away from the stagnated trance many live in
all wondering why things are still the same
playing this blame game to hide their personal shames
and deflect responsibility to those without accountability
yet inaction only derails oneself
from what could be but is not
because of what can't be
without action
while staying alive is merely a fraction
of what life is all about
because free-will gives us all the freedom to make choices
to end silence and use our voices for is wanted
to continue to pray and go get what is already promised
because this life is about living

and how one chooses to live it
as we are our experiences
with the choice to choose
what we experiencing
so why play this blame game
when it only assures
your life will remain the same
and you remain just another name
making false claims about dreams you don't work for
saying you want more
but doing nothing to get it
point fingers for the emptiness you feeling
blame the gun maker for the killing
the addict for the dealing
the people at the top despite you ignoring your opportunities
playing the blame game to cover up your lack of priorities
and making excuses by coming up with more stories
yet all that talking can't and won't get you any where
except right there where you started
until you depart from blaming
and start aiming for higher expectations of your own making
no one can enslave you unless you allow it
because you are more powerful than you may ever know
yet only through hard work could you ever show
to yourself and the world how far you can go
if you just take responsibility
and allow yourself to exceed life's impossibilities.

Your light... R.I.P. Nycee Harris

as the sun sets on your life,

it is your light that still shines through

for in your weakest hour it was you who gave me life

and taught me how to appreciate life,

 despite the inevitable end of your own

despite knowing God was preparing a place for you

you never allowed the cancer to take the best of you

still and always willing to give me, your friend, the best of you.

and though i may be hurting here on this earth without you

it is the light you left behind that makes it easier to go on with out you

because you taught me so much by simply smiling

and i discovered my own light by smiling back at you

and now i smile randomly at just the thought of you

and though i'm missing you,

i know i'm better because i knew you

i know i'm better because your light shined on me

and now i'm better because i allow your light to shine through me

"I dedicate **'Your light...'** to Nycee Harris. I truly miss you my friend. I miss your laughter, your crazy sense of humor, and your bright smile the most. Thank you for sharing your light with me. I am forever grateful God blessed me with the time we did have together. I love you and I always will." ~Indy

PTSD...

post fire that awakened the day early

yet i still see it all vividly

and hear screaming so loudly it feels like the cries of a broken mother are still right next to me

and the look on her face is still staring right through me

as she succumbed to the moment when she learned the very fire that awaken the day early had taken her son

a **traumatic** tragedy that should have never happened

but when the smoke cleared the inevitable had happened

yet it hasn't gotten any easier to fully digest what has happened

because he was

confined, constrained, consumed by a fire he could not escape

and now i am

confined, constrained, consumed by the nightmare i can't awake from

of his final moment

a moment i can't forget

a moment i still see

stress lines suggest i'm not properly adjusting to the moment

because when i dream i still see the moment

and i want nothing more than to forget the moment

but not forget you

just your final moment

an all too familiar moment i wish was just a nightmare i could wake up from

only the **disorder** of my nights remind me of what was once there and the drive by each morning reminds me it really happened

and it wasn't a nightmare i can't seem to wake up from

the fire was real

an innocent life was lost

because he was

consumed by a fire

and i am now

consumed by a nightmare i can't wake up from

Who loves me? Why me? What is my purpose? Where am I going? Why did that happen? What is love? Is this it? Which direction do I go? Who do I turn to? Does anyone hear me? Does anyone see me? Am I changing? Have I changed? How much have I really grown? Who am I? How important is faith? What really matters? How important is love? Why don't they love me? What is the motive? What is love's purpose? What is a valid question? What is the point of curiosity? What is the purpose of learning? Why do I write? Why did I start writing? Who do I write for? What purpose do I write for? What purpose does my writing serve? What is the lesson? Does age matter? Who is God? What did the experience reveal? Is God real? Can I really be myself? How did society get here? What is perception? What is it to become of tomorrow? What does the future hold? Who is going to help the kids? Why do we hate more than we love? What do I want to be? What do I want to accomplish? What will it take to get there? Is the sky my limit? What will I be remembered for? Why do I share my poetry? Who is my inspiration? What is my inspiration? Is it time to let go? How much time do I have left? What do I regret?

What is the meaning of life? What is truth? How do I get to Heaven? Is love ever forever? Am I dreaming? Is this real? What is an illusion? Why am I hurting? Why do I care? Who do I admire? What is a friend? What is the meaning of family? What is fear? Am I afraid or cautious? Why do I pray? Are prayers really heard? Can I love again? How do I forgive? How do I move past the pain? Can I forgive her? Can I forgive him? What is a mother? What is a father? What is success? Where does my peace come from? Why do I smile? Can I trust her? Can I trust him? Why a book?

what really matters?

love?

faith?

service?

matters:

Be of importance; have significance

A subject of concern, feeling, or action

friendship?

family?

wealth?

The role of hope...

hope is the key to satisfied living

the key that keeps us all believing

that hard work keeps us on the receiving end

of achieving all the things we believe in

hope is our way of telling a friend

that troubled times won't last to the end

that brighter days are on the horizon

and God ensures those who believe in him that no man ever has to stand on an island alone

hope is the motivation that keeps us growing

that keeps us wanting to know more

and see more of the view not easily seen

but obtainable when hope accompanies our dreams

hope is everything you need to fully believe in yourself

to believe even when you're the only one standing up

God got you and you got yourself

hope is our dreams

the ones we sometimes have to defer

yet hope allows us to remain undeterred

knowing there must be something better waiting

as God awaits the day to present it

hope is assurance

that no matter how down you get

despite how bad times get

God won't quit unless you do

hope is assurance

that every day is an opportunity

to take one more step

let go of one more regret

and get the best out each moment

hope is our faith in God

for those who fully believe he will provide for them

and trust that every day he works our behalf

even on days when life appears to be moving too fast

and it becomes harder to keep the focus

hope is what reassures us we are chosen for only that which God knows
we are strong enough to bear

Ode to my brother...

ode to my brother whose heart surpasses the definition of
unconditional love
and is always willing to give of himself even when it is undeserved

ode to my brother who sees life with eyes that reflect the innocence of
children
and insists love be given without pre-conditions

ode to my brother who does not bask in hate
and believes each new day is a day to offer forgiveness

ode to my brother who surpasses his medically diagnosed limitations
and exceeds the world's expectations every day

ode to my brother supposedly born to fit in
yet lives his life every day by standing out

ode to my brother supposedly challenged by learning
but always yearning to grow more and know more
so he learns more than previously expected

ode to my brother who teaches me what it means to love
unconditionally by loving me without conditions

ode to my brother who has loved me
since we were children
and has always been the big brother willing to listen

ode to my brother who captured my heart before my first word
and loves me more than i sometimes feel i deserve

"I dedicate **'Ode to my brother...'** to my big-little brother, Arthur Byers Jr. The love and kindness you continue to show me and this world despite the evil and wickedness that we have both been through is a love I strive daily to imitate. Thank you for loving me despite my ways and giving me a real-world example of unconditional love. I love you and I always will." ~Indy

I am a survivor of child abuse...

i was once a victim of child abuse
reduced to something lesser than myself
i was stripped of my youth
and introduced to adulthood before my childhood was over
yet i now i accept it was me who allowed the pain to take me over

though i make no excuse, nor excuse the actions of my momma
but i had to forgive my momma before i could stop blaming myself
i had to see past my own pain to realize i wasn't the only one hurting
i had to accept my own blame to realize i wasn't the only one broken
and i had to grow up to realize my experiences, both good & bad, were
for a greater purpose

because my momma isnt perfect
yet my momma did what she could
maybe not what she should have
or what i wished she would have done
instead, my momma did what she knew
when she made me a victim of the same maltreatment and beatings she
was exposed to
the same physical abuse and emotional neglect she was accustomed to
but i am no longer a victim

i am a victor
while the path of my life was the path to victory
a path shaped by things that are draining to even think about
of a time when a smile and school was the least i had to worry about
and only a few even asked what my tears were about.

but i'm here today,
no longer a victim of child abuse

no, i am a survivor of child abuse

no longer ashamed of my truth

because i now understand its roots

i now stand as an example of a good seed sprouted from a tainted fruit

a rose that grew from beneath the smothering weight of concrete

no longer retreating behind the shadows of yesterday

today i embrace the light that has guided me all along when anger
threatened my sight

i now stand today no longer contained by my past

but forever changed by my past

now understanding my momma was the first to be abused

therefore she only did what she knew

unable to separate her own pain from the pain she took me through

unable to abstain from her emotional eruptions

unable to change what had become so ingrained in her

therefore i no longer place the blame on her

i only cry for my momma because i was once a victim just like her

All children matter...

yes i am only a child
but like all children,
i matter too
so maybe i'm not the tallest
or even the smallest
but i know you greatest owner in nba history me
or maybe your not caring keeps you from seeing me
tho i'm the one suffering when you choose to ignore me
i'm the one who is exploited when no one protects me
and no one hears me when it's so easy to pretend i don't matter
but i do

and i need guidance just as much as any other kid
because love should never be just for the other kids,
the white kids, the tall kids,
the smart kids, the straight kids
wait, what?
yes, the straight kids
that learn from adults how to make life tough for the gay kids like me

and when no steps in to stop it,
it sends the message there is no need to stop it because i don't matter
but i do
so why is society telling me i'm different?
why have i been made to feel different every day of my short-lived
existence?
why is society insisting my rights be different?
my freedoms be different?
why and how am i different from you?
when like all children, i matter too

yet i am a only child already dreading growing up
while other gay kids like myself choose not to grow up
because adult life doesn't look much better for us
when as kids we're taught everyone else is better than us
treated like everyone is better than us
some even use the bible to say the others better than us

when if you cared to notice, you'd see my life is rough enough
because i'm trying to figure out my personal identity
while trying to figure out a sexuality identity
that comes with a sexual attraction that chose me
so understand, i didn't get a choice in the matter
but like all children, i matter too

and if you really wanted to, you could stop judging me
offending me, hurting me
because all those things you say and do take their toll on me
when the things you say and do should be to support me
encourage me, love me
like any other child, any other person
because i am only a child
but like all children, i matter too!

> "I dedicate **'All children matter...'** to each
> and every child in this world. Despite your
> age, race, gender, size, shape, wealth,
> talent, intelligence, and sexual orientation,
> I want you all to know that you DO
> matter! We are all children of God and He
> loves us all despite our differences." ~Indy

Be you...

society says be you,

then they judge you

but i say be you

because i love you

not because i have to

but because i want to

not because of what i know about you

or can get out of you

but because of the smile i occasionally get to see when i'm around you

so smile more

and worry less about opinions, stereotypes, and other's expectations of you

because no one wears the same shoes as you

and no one has walked the same path as you

so let no one tell you how best to be you

because their opinions only hold true if you allow it

so when society says be you

simply respond "i am & will be"

though they may still judge you

let them know God is the judge of you

and you are the only one capable of being you

a unique you

a beautiful you

a you that no one else can be

know you're amazing as you are

and in time you will be even more amazing than present day

know you're special just as you are

and in time the world will see and know just how special you are

know you're beautiful

and in time your beauty will only become more beautiful

as you continue to discover

and continue to grow

because you are what you have experienced

but most importantly, you are what you are willing to be

so be not deterred by society's judgments

but know i love you for simply being you...

*"I dedicate **'Be you...'** to all my readers, supporters, family, friends, professors, classmates, co-workers, social network followers & friends, and anyone else I may have missed. It is because of all of you I was able to complete my book and I am forever grateful for the roles each and every one of you have played in my life and in the completion of this collection. ~Indy*

ABOUT THE AUTHOR

Writing and poetry have been the lone constants in the life of Natashia "Indy" Easley. Originally from Birmingham, AL, Indy's poetry reflects a life that has taken her from the country of Montezuma, GA to the city streets of Atlanta back to her hometown of Birmingham. It was back in Birmingham where Indy was inspired and motivated to share her words and voice with the world. While writing has always been a natural ability, her skills as a poet have evolved throughout her life as she has overcome struggle, pain, and heartache. Holding a Bachelor's degree in Technical & Professional Communication from Southern Polytechnic State University and a Master's degree in Social Work from The University of Alabama, Indy's personal poetry and her career as a Social Worker both reflect her two strongest passions in life: personal expression and service to others. Indy currently resides in Birmingham, AL and works as a workshop facilitator for Real Life Poets, Inc.

www.ingramcontent.com/pod-product-compliance
Lightning Source LLC
Chambersburg PA
CBHW060513030426
42337CB00015B/1873